My Precious Gift

Poems and Photography by

Dawn Teresa McKinney

To order additional copies of this book, contact:
Xlibris
844-714-8691
www.Xlibris.com
Orders@Xlibris.com

ISBN: Softcover   978-1-4568-2139-5
        EBook   979-8-3694-3690-5

Print information available on the last page

Rev. date: 12/16/2024

Acknowledgements

To my wonderful mother Teresa Dawn McKinney for supporting me through my ups and downs. For being the encouraging person I needed to get these poems finally published. Thank you so much, I love you.

To my grandparents Dana and Wanda McKinney, thank you for your love and support. Thank you for always being there for me.

To my cousin Samantha Lynn Millage, thank you for your love, support, and being such wonderful inspiration for me. You are a special light in my life and I am so grateful for the times we have spent together, I love you.

To my cousins Dana Michelle Kittendorf and Tamara Cornett, thank you for getting your books published first. It was a good push in getting this book published. I love you both and I hope you enjoy it.

To my special friend, Sarbelia Muniz growing up with you has been such a joy in my life; we are so close, we are more like sisters than friends. I love you and your family so much. Thank you for always being there for me.

I love all of my family and friends and thank you from the bottom of my heart for all your love and support.

IN MEMORY OF

Uncle Dana Alan McKinney, Aunt Sandra Jones, Great-Aunt Rosa Maciejczyk, Great-Grandpa William "Big Papaw" Lucas and my Great-Grandma Mollie "Mamaw" Lucas; Even though Mamaw passed away a couple of months before my birth, I feel our connection with our passion for poetry.

Milagros "Mama" Rosa who was a loving babysitter that I considered a grandmother;
"Con tu adios, te llevas mi Corazon"

Table of Contents

FAMILY
TIES

Beyond the Tall Trees   Sebring, FL

Dana

He closes his eyes
And all he sees
Is what lies
Beyond the tall, tall trees

Beyond the tall, tall trees,
There is a golden sun.
Shining so brightly,
On his son

On his son with his mind he sees,
His son having so much fun,
Running and jumping and
Laughing so freely

Running and jumping and
Laughing so freely,
Is the way we all should be here
Though he is in a place with no fears or tears,
He will always, always be near.

Always be near, he will be
Next to him as an angel he appears.
To help and heal,
All the pain he feels.

From losing his only son,
Named Dana!

-2001-

Good Morning   Lake Placid, FL

Mama

Still,
I can hear her say, Ven aqui, Dawnee!
I can see her standing, with arms wide open for me to hug.
I can smell the Spanish food that she would make.
I can taste the candy she would give us kids around Christmas time.
I remember the prayers she said at night.

Still,
I can hear her laughing, at the TV shows.
I can see her watching Sesame street with us.
I can smell the shampoo she used to wash our hair with.
I can taste the coffee she made me at times.
I remember never wanting to leave her side.

Still,
I can hear her teaching me, how to speak Spanish.
I can see her face, when I close my eyes.
I can smell the medicine she would put on our wounds.
I can taste the treats she always had around.
I remember these things, more and more each and every day.

She was not just a babysitter,
But more like a grandmother.
Part of me is sad that she had to go away
But I know she is in Heaven,
Still watching over us,
Until we meet again.

In dedication to Milagros Rosa

-2002-

5

My Ginger Girl

I was given Ginger when I was a little girl.
When she looked up at me with her big brown eyes,
And stood by my side with the tallest of pride,
I knew right then she'd be with me for a long, long time.

She brightened every child's heart,
And protected all the ones she loved.
She helped all animals find their way,
Also some humans along just the same

I liked to believe that she was a ballerina in her past life,
Because she would run around in circles,
With strides of ease,
And never did she get herself dizzy.

She was my best friend,
And when my world seemed so crazy,
She would put her paw on my hand,
To let me know she was there for me.

As the years went on,
She pushed herself to stay so strong.
But she grew older and her runs turned into slow walks,
Unfortunately, she lost that struggle when she passed away in an early spring.

A couple of years later,
I was approached by a young man that said,
I don't remember your name ma'am,
But you lived in a house on Meade Street with Ginger.

I smiled as I watched his expressions,
As he told his buddies some stories about her,
I felt so sad to let him know,
She had passed away a few years ago.

His smiles quickly turned into tears,
As he said, she was the only light in my dark childhood.
Watching and playing with her was such a delight,
I'm sorry for our loss; she'll forever be in my heart.

I smiled as tears streamed down my face,
Thinking how lucky I had been to have my life so graced.
Her dedication to each of us, young and old,
That is a feeling I will treasure and keep with me always.

Ginger girl was sent to watch over us like our own little guardian angel.
She blessed everyone's life in one way or another.
She will always be in my heart and,
Her funny personality will live in my memories for the rest of my life.

I am so glad to have shared such wonderful times,
With an amazing companion,
That I miss so much everyday,
Known to lots of people as my dog,
Ginger!

-2010-

Saint Sunset   St. Petersburg, FL

My Precious Gift

On July 30, 1980, I received such a wonderful gift.
I got something that you don't come across very often.
I decided to give it a whirl,
Even though, it came in a form I didn't accept.

This precious gift is my mother.

It is rare that you get a gift that will help you through thick and thin.
Who has a love so unconditional,
Who is beautiful on the outside as well as within,
And who is never one to be so traditional.

This precious gift is my mother.

She is my strength when I am weak.
She gives me courage when I am afraid.
She is my calm when I am tempered.
She is my protector when I am in danger.
She is who I consider to be my living angel.
She is my only true friend that I will love to all eternities end.

This precious gift is my mother.

She has played many parts in my life,
Like being a father figure by scaring away bad boyfriends and teaching me how to slow dance.
She has been a big brother by showing me how to shoot a three-pointer and how to score a touchdown.
She has been a big sister by telling me about boys and how to put make-up on.
She has been a best friend when I have needed someone to talk to and to have a girl's night out.

This precious gift is my mother.

M is for the many times she has hugged and kissed me hi and good-bye.
O is for being so open-minded and having a reasonable opinion.
T is for the trust she has in me to do what I think is right.
H is for having such a big heart and being so kind.
E is for the exciting times we have shared.
R is for being really down to earth.

This precious gift is my mother.

She and I have a bond so great,
Not even a step-father could break.
She isn't like most mothers I know,
She is never distant nor is one to smother.
Some call her the coolest mom on the block,
That would make you laugh with a hand puppet made of a sock.

This precious gift is my mother.

When she says, I love you
I know she means it from the bottom of her heart.
I can not believe, I ended up the luckiest person on earth,
To have the best mother a girl could ask for.
About 21 years ago, I received the most precious gift in the whole world.
And I surely thank God,
For my precious gift that
I call my mom.

This precious gift is my mother.

This most precious gift is my dear sweet mother.

-2002-

Samantha

She is the cutest thing,
That you could ever see.
With her unique shaped eye,
That change color from the greenest shade of an emerald,
To the bluest of the skies.

She likes to have fun,
With dancing, cheering, and laughing so much,
I love to see her ever so happy,
When she says, come out play with me Aunt Dawnee!

At the little age of seven,
She is so smart.
She likes to play games,
Like Candyland, Sorry, and Hide and Seek.

She is always playful,
But has her quiet moments too,
Especially, when she is asleep,
She looks like an angel on a small cloud way up high.

The only time I see her frown,
Is when I have to leave her until we meet next time,
Sometimes she says the darnedest things,
This makes me think,
What goes on in her inquisitive mind?

She shines ever so brightly,
With her bubbly personality.
She lights up the room,
With her beautiful smile!

I love her so dearly,
As does everyone else,
Who has met this bundle of joy,
That I proudly call my cousin,
Samantha!

-2002-

St. Stills   St. Petersburg, FL

Remember Him This Way

Remember him…
    Standing about six feet high,
    With white blonde hair,
    And gorgeous blue eyes.
Remember him…
    With the brightest smile,
    To light my darkest night.
    Having the biggest hug,
    On a Christmas morning light.

Remember Him This Way

Remember him…
    Having the top grades in the class,
    With knowledge of great mass.
    Teaching others what he knows,
    While astonishing teachers to and fro'.
Remember him…
    As the son every parent dreamed of having,
    As a little brother his big sister looked up to,
    And the uncle who loved this niece dearly,
    For he is no longer with us on this earth,
    But up in heaven waiting to see us again.

Remember Him This Way

In dedication to Dana Alan McKinney

-2002-

Entertaining

I Like You

I like the way you move your hips.
I like your smooth and luscious lips.
I like the way you hold me close.
I like the way you don't want to let me go.

I like you!

I like the color of your eyes.
I like the way that you smile.
I like your passionate kisses.
I like the way you listen.

I like you!

I like the way you touch my face.
I like the little moans that you make.
I like the way we talk all night long.
I like the way you are so polite.

I like you!

I like you for who you are inside.
I like the way I can show you my shy side.
I like the way you call me sweetie.
I like it best when you are near me.
I like you a whole lot and hope you like me just as much!

-2002-

My Calling

Little did I know?
When I started this show,
That I would find my call,
In HHS Varsity football!

I patched up the player,
In bandages of layers,
While other girls went to balls,
And hung out at the malls

The guys have been funny
And sometimes as sweet as honey
But after all the endless drills,
I can say it has been a big thrill!

-1997-

The Groundbreaking Game

As the cheerleaders shouted,
Go! Fight! Win!
The team blew into town like a leaf in the wind.
Their faces were all so serious and one hit from them would make you delirious!

As the fans started to cheer,
They strutted their way on the field.
As the opponents cowardly drew their heads down,
Our captain boastfully said, "Don't worry we'll let you get one touchdown!"

As the helmets went to crashing,
The running backs ran as fast as lightning.
When the score would raise higher and higher,
The other teams' faces grew lower and lower.

Even our band was far better than theirs.
Just listen and see for yourselves.
Our mascot, The Spartan Man
Tamed those Mustangs'

As the time clock wound down
The opposite side started to frown
And the sweet smell of victory
Made those Mustangs HISTORY!

And to the Mustangs
See you next year
'Cause tonight is the night we're gonna get down and cheer....

Go Spartans!
Go Spartans!
Go! Go!
Go Spartans!
-1996-

The Mayor's Cup

It looked like sunshine in the forecast,
As the stadium filled up so fast
All of the fans came fully prepared,
With their painted faces and dyed hair.

The anticipation as game time approached,
Nearly gave the coaches a stroke.
The football players came out shouting,
Let's kick some Bulldogs' butts!
While the opponents laughed and replied,
They are not so tough.

They showed no fear,
As the knees got bruised,
The eyes black and blue,
The arms broken left and right,
Some even got hit so hard they saw a big bright light.

The trainers told them not to play,
But they wanted to stay in anyway.
They threw a little dirt on their wounds,
And played to the very end

At the end of the game,
They all got together and sang,
We are the CHAMPIONS!
The cheerleaders shook the opponents' hands,
While the crowd ran out from the stands

This win broke a fifteen-year losing streak,
And now the Bulldogs know the Spartans are not weak.
As the senior football players broke out in tears,
They told the underclass good luck next year.

-1997-

Imagination

Almost Heaven

There is a place far away

Where the children can laugh and play all day

It is made up of mostly meadows and forests,

With horse carriages to take you on your course

It has the bluest of skies,

With great castles way up high,

The greenest of grass

And mountains of mass

It is slightly larger than West Virginia,

But has no snakes like they do in India.

The fill up their mugs with green beer

They hang out in pubs to dance and cheer

While telling myths and stories,

About famous saints and all their glories,

Just thinking of this beautiful place

Brings a smile to my face

-1998-

Ever Flowing Winter Haven, FL

My Safe Place

Escape with me
Into my dreams
A place where there are no lines
None to be crossed or
To be walked on

It is filled with the brightest of colors
Purples, blues, yellows, and greens
And scattering about are
Fairies, dragons, and sleeping unicorns

As you enter this place, magical dust
Gets sprinkled all over
To protect you
From any bad spells that might linger

There are no bad, mean, or evil ones allowed
If they get through we scream out loud
And the fierce dragon comes out to our rescue
They get rid,
Rid of all the evil ones

This is a place we go to
Laugh and play
Sing and dance
Fly and soar
Flutter about
Like there is no tomorrow
There really is no tomorrow
Or today in this place
It just exists

Why keep track of time when you having fun

This is my safe place
Do you have one?

-2002-

The Furious Storm

That night was so frightening
With the crashing of the lightning
The pounding of the thunder
Woke me from my slumber

The drops of blue, black rain,
Came pouring down on the window pane.
The roaring of the winds
Scared away all the chickens

Look, there goes the old oak tree
Where we use to play hide and go seek
And isn't that the neighbor's car
Sitting on top of the town bar

The breaking of the glass,
Hit me so fast.
I passed out from a bleeding vein
And woke up in such awful, pain

I took a look around
And there was no one to be found
Only the debris on the ground
Lost in the middle of somewhere

But didn't know where

-1998-

Garden Falls   Winter Haven, FL

Infatuation

Lake Sunrise   *Lake Placid, FL*

Candle Light

The flickering of a candle light
Is blown out by the winds of the night
She says, if he doesn't feel the love I have for thee,
Then it isn't meant to be.

A voice from within her says....

But wait! This isn't right!
The candle is to burn all night
So my love can find his way home.

A pause in her voice....

But if my love cannot find is way home
Without the guide of the light nor my love,
Then it isn't meant to be.

It just wasn't meant to be.

-1995-

Before Dawn   Lake Placid, FL

My Soul Mate

The man I fall in love with will know we were meant to be together at first site.

He will look deep into my brown eyes and with no surprise find the love of his life.

The man I fall in love with can make me smile once in awhile and turn my frowns upside down.

He will chase all my blues away and when I'm sick he'll stay with me all day.

The man I fall in love with can make me laugh until I cry and then dry the tears from my eyes.

The man I fall in love with is a man I will love until I die and that is no lie.

The man I fall in love with will make my life complete.

And he is waiting somewhere out there for me.

The man I fall in love with is whom I want by my side.

The man I fall in love with is who I need.

His soul and my soul will unite to become soul mates for life.

-1999-

My Love & Lust

There is one that I love
And long to be loved by.
Then there is one I lust,
And long to be lusted by.

What do I do when the one I love is far away?
And the one that I lust is close but waiting for someone else?
Why do I love this person, now that he is so far away?
Why does the one I lust, lust another?

Oh! Why did I fall in love?
Oh! Why did I flirt with my friend?

The love and lust of my life are one and the same.
But he is somewhere else and is waiting for someone other than me.
If only he knew the things that I feel
If only I could give one kiss to show him what I feel is real.

There is one that I love and one I lust
But they are one and the same.
The only man I could ever truly trust

I wish to see him again.

The love and lust of my life
Are one and the same

-1996-

Mystery Man

Sitting here looking into the eyes of a mystery

Imagining all the possible palaces, peasants, princes, and princesses we would see together

Seeing this mystery man dressed up so nice, I'm

Thinking of a hundred ways to say what I feel inside

Listening to the deep voice of this mystery man keeps me,

Trying to learn as much as I can about this mysterious person

Feeling over-whelmed with sensual emotions that make me burst like a volcano

Sensing that he feels the same way and wants me not to stay away

Crying good tears of pleasure when I am near him,

Dreaming of this enchantingly, fine mystery man is,

Keeping my mind occupied and my heart,

Fluttering like a butterfly,

Splashing like a dolphin,

Flickering like a candle light, and

Loving as a morning ocean.

-2002-

LIFE
LESSONS

Choices

Standing here in front of two long pathways,

Both with my potential future

A tall shadow hangs over my shoulders as I ponder.

All of their conclusions come to going down the left side

No one is telling me to go right

Maybe the left pathway will be the one for me,

But I have to take control of my own future.

I will choose the

Right!

And if I screw up at least I can honestly say it was my choice.

-2000-

Sunset Road   Sebring, FL

Finding My Place

Standing here looking around
Trying to find a place to belong
Seeing nothing but the old same faces
Keeps me wondering, wondering about new places

As the days go by,
Still I try,

To find a peaceful place
That would bring a smile to my face.
Dreaming of a blue and purple sky,
Somewhere way up high,

A place where it doesn't matter the color of my skin
A beautiful location where I could fit in
I guess that place exists only in my mind
So I will just close my eyes and there I'll find

The place I want to be
Always in my daydreams!

-2001-

My Old Neighborhood

Amanda was my friend who was the daredevil that did the things not even the boys would attempt. She was like the sister I never had.
Angela had the most beautiful eyes and complexion I've ever seen.

Big Jimmy was tall, blonde, blue-eyed hunk who my mom picked up from school everyday.
Brad was ever so fine in his white tees and tight blue jeans.
Brandy was the new girl on the block who was older, mature, more experienced and developed than me and my other friends.

Carrie was the friend with the real singing talent. She always attracted a crowd.
Charlie and Edna was a sweet old couple who never complained much and always lent a helping hand.
Christina was the prissy and sensitive friend and had moments were she would drive me up the walls, but I never said anything about it because I didn't want to hurt her feelings.

Hong was the nice Vietnamese woman who lived across the way.

Jimmy was Carrie's younger brother, but you would never think they were related due to his constant crave to cause trouble.
Javier was Julia's younger brother. He was always shy and quiet.
Julia was sweet and always came to my mom with a cat to take in. She also had long, long hair that felt and looked like a horse's mane.
Julio and I didn't get along much cause he loved to terrorize me. He was a big bully.

Kenny was a short guy with the attitude of a macho man.

Lori was a beautiful model type of a girl with long brown hair and brown eyes. I would always hear her playing songs by Jon Bon Jovi.

Mark was a cute guy with a heart of gold and Irish pride.

Ozzie was who I had little crushes on and as I grew older it turned into love.

Randy was tall, with long black hair, kind of mysterious and such a shy guy.
Reynier was who I love playing cops and robbers Miami Vice style with and he is still a good friend to this day.
Ricky was the practical joker; especially, around Halloween. He left too soon, may he Rest in Peace.
Robert was Reynier's older brother that I wrote my first, I Love You, note to.

Sherry was always bright-eyed and bushy-tailed just like the fuzzy bunnies she would to show me.
Sonny was who the second love note went to.

Toni and **E**d were Amanda's grandparents and whom I considered family. They were fun to be around. May the both of them, Rest in Peace, as well.

These were people from my old neighborhood.

Who have in one way or another have taught me a lot about differences.

Differences make the world interesting and life worth living.

I will always treasure growing up on Meade Street and never forget my old neighborhood.

-2002-

The Pier   Sebring, FL

The Pier

The sun is making its way through to shine ever so brightly on you.
The stillness of the lake is calming me to my soul.
This feeling will stay with me wherever I go.
The beaming rays of light bounce and stray as in fright,
The echoing sound of the birds goes out so far so it can be heard.

Out on the pier, just before the sun goes to bed!

Those in love take a walk,
They come here often just to talk.
They hold one another by the hand and kiss each other before the day ends.
It seems so close yet so far from the opposite side, a place where people come to hide,
Hide away from all the commotion and confusion, it is an instant meditation

Out on the pier, just before the sun goes to bed

When I think of where I have been, where I am going and what is left to do
When I am just plain doubtful, I go back to the pier and all of my troubles start to disappear.

Out on the pier, just before the sun goes to bed

-2002-

Saying Good Bye

I left my hometown,
To find new ground
I wanted to start with a new slate.
Instead, all I got was more on my plate.

I came to a small town,
To get away from the city.
To wake up to a peaceful sound,
In the woods, where it is quite pretty.

Though, I miss my friends more and more,
I long for them to hug and hold.
Remembering the times, keeps me happy,
Happiness is what I yearn for,
And home is where it is.

I know times are different,
And people have changed.
But so have I,
So I guess this is good-bye!

-2001-

Too Many Hurdles

Casey woke up with a yawn,
At the crack of the dawn
After getting dressed,
She ate her breakfast.
Instead of going outside to play,
She had to work hard all day.
She started by brushing the hair
Of her mare,
Meanwhile wishing she was elsewhere.

Even though, her bedroom was filled with colorful ribbons
And first place trophies six feet high,
The only thing Casey could do was cry.
She rode and jumped and sometimes fell,
But got up quickly
So her father would not yell.
Her father entered her in contest after contest,
Until she finally broke down and confessed,

Hurdle Racing was your dream, dad.
Not mine,
I am only nine, dad.

I am only nine!

-1999-

43

Photograph Locations

Summer Sunset-The cover photo was taken in July of 2000. The location was at Lake Jackson in Sebring, FL.

Beyond the Tall Trees-This photo was taken in October of 2010. The location was off of State Road 66 in Sebring, FL.

Good Morning- This photo was taken in November of 2010. The location was at Lake Placid in Lake Placid, FL.

Saint Sunset-This photo was taken in December of 2008. The location was in Saint Petersburg, FL.

St. Stills-This photo was taken in December of 2008. The location was in Saint Petersburg, FL.

Ever Flowing-This photo was taken in May of 2008. The location was at Cypress Gardens Adventure Park in Winter Haven, FL.

Garden Falls-This photo was taken in May of 2008. The location was at Cypress Gardens Adventure Park in Winter Haven, FL.

Lake Sunrise- This photo was taken in November 2010. The location was at Lake Placid in Lake Placid, FL.

Before Dawn- This photo was taken in November 2010. The location was at Lake Placid in Lake Placid, FL.

Sunset Road-This photo was taken in October of 2010. The location was off of State Road 66 in Sebring, FL.

The Pier-This photo was taken in July of 2000. The location was at The Pier at Lake Jackson in Sebring, FL.

Printed in the United States
by Baker & Taylor Publisher Services